# Easy Graded Organ Music

## Book Two

*Compiled by Robert Gower*

*Edited by C. H. Trevor*

Music Department
OXFORD UNIVERSITY PRESS
Oxford and New York

6-95.

# CONTENTS

# COMPILER'S NOTE

These two volumes of easy graded organ music represent the best pieces from C. H. Trevor's Organ Books 1–6 and are designed to provide a selection of practical, accessible, and enjoyable pieces for players who take up the instrument. Some of the shorter pieces are included to improve technical security, while the more substantial ones explore musical interpretation and provide material suitable both for use in services and occasions of broader appeal. The pieces in each book are arranged in order of difficulty, so that a feeling of steady progress can develop. Fingering, pedalling, and registration have been pared down to a minimum to encourage discussion of style between teacher and pupils, and to avoid being prescriptive.

Caleb Henry Trevor (1895–1976) was organist of Lincoln's Inn Chapel, and professor of organ at the Royal Academy of Music. He was a fine recitalist (it was his series of broadcast recitals in 1935 that first drew British attention to the music of Max Reger), but perhaps most influential as a distinguished organ teacher. At the age of 65 Trevor stopped giving recitals and began to produce a series of publications for Oxford University Press, including the *Oxford Organ Method*. They were hugely influential on a generation of performers and students. In some ways Trevor's interest in earlier composers was ahead of his time, and his fascinating collections of unknown music did much to revolutionize the organist's repertoire. Perhaps his unique gift was in finding pieces that took account of the needs of ordinary organists and students without ever compromising musical quality.

In presenting this collection, one can only reinforce Trevor's favourite maxim: 'always play like a musician.'

ROBERT GOWER
*Radley College, 1995*

# SONATA PER ORGANO

Giovanni Battista Bassani (1657–1716)

The original is, as above, on two staves. The indications for the use of the pedal are the composer's.

Ped.

# ANDANTE WITH VARIATIONS

Felix Mendelssohn (1809–1847)

# Hymnus, 'VEXILLA REGIS PRODEUNT'

John Bull (1562–1628)

Originally for manuals alone.

# Chorale prelude, 'VATER UNSER IM HIMMELREICH'

D. Buxtehude (1637–1707)

# PRAELUDIUM

Johann Krieger (1651–1735)

14

# Chorale prelude, 'ACH GOTT, ERHOR MEIN SEUFZEN UND WEHKLAGEN'

Johann Ludwig Krebs (1713–1780)

# TRIO (Op. 49 No. 10)

Josef Rheinberger (1839–1901)

# PRELUDE AND FUGUE IN F MINOR

Johann Ludwig Krebs (1713–1780)

20

# POSTLUDE

Alexandre Guilmant (1837–1911)

23

**Tempo primo**

26

# Chorale Prelude, "EIN' FESTE BURG IST UNSER GOTT'"

Max Reger (1873–1916)

**Moderato**

# TRIO IN C MINOR

Johann Ludwig Krebs (1713–1780)

# TRIO IN A MINOR

Johann Ludwig Krebs (1713–1780)

# Chorale Prelude, 'O EWIGKEIT, DU DONNERWORT'

Johann Ludwig Krebs (1713–1780)

# Chorale prelude, 'ACH GOTT, VERLASS MICH NICHT'

Max Reger (1873–1916)

# TRIO DU SIXIÈME TON

Jacques Boyvin (1653–1706)

# CANON IN C (Op. 56 No. 1)

Robert Schumann (1810–1856)

# CANON IN B MINOR (Op. 56 No. 5)

Robert Schumann (1810–1856)

Manual indications are editorial. If the organ is a 2-manual, the parts indicated for the Choir should be played on the Great.

44

Reproduced and printed by
Halstan & Co. Ltd., Amersham, Bucks., England